CALLING

GOD

TO SILENCE

WITCHCRAFT

POWERS

By

Tella Olayeri

+2348023583168

Published By:

GOD'S LINK VENTURES

Email tellaolayeri@gmail.com

Website www.tellaolayeri.com

Blog www.tellaolayeri.com/blog

US Contact
Ruth Jack
14 Milewood Road
Verbank
N.Y.12585
U.S.A. +19176428989

All texts, calls, letters, testimonies and enquiries are welcome.

CONNECT WITH US

FACEBOOK

(Like and follow our page)

https://web.facebook.com/tellaolayeri/

(Join our Facebook Group)

Do you want your dream interpreted, do you need powerful morning and night prayers that command breakthrough, healing and favour.

Join my Facebook group today and receive testimony.

https://web.facebook.com/groups/tellaolayeri

INSTAGRAM

https://www.instagram.com/tellaolayeri/

TWITTER

https://twitter.com/tellaolayeri

DEDICATION

This book is dedicated to the **HOLY GHOST** for inspiring me to write this eye opening book.

APPRECIATION

My appreciation goes to my dedicated wife, **MRS NGOZI OLAYERI,** who typed the manuscript of this book and designed the cover page. My darling wife I say thank you. My appreciation equally goes to my lovely children, **MISS IBUKUN, DAVID, MICHAEL COMFORT and MERCY.** They encouraged me day and night as I write this book

Respect and honor should be given to who is due. Favor comes from God and men as well. My calling (writing evangelism) met the timely support of a particular man of God, preacher, teacher, prophet and General Overseer. He awakes my inner man and gave me sound spiritual support. Without his earlier support for my first book, <u>Fire for Fire Prayer Book</u> and subsequent ones, I may not be where I am today in Christian literature writing. He gallantly stood by me in fulfillment of my calling.

This book you are holding is a testimony of my claim. This book wouldn't have seen the light of the day, if not for the spiritual encouragement I gathered from my father in the Lord who served as spiritual mirror that brightens my hope to explore my calling.

I am talking of no any other person than the **General Overseer of MOUNTAIN OF FIRE AND MIRACLES MINISTRIES WORLD WIDE, DR. D. K. OLUKOYA.**

Once again, I say thank you sir. Your support has yielded yet another earth shaking book.

THANKS.
Evangelist Tella Olayeri.

PREFACE

There is no way witchcraft power can contend with your life and glory if you know right tools to apply in every situation. Prayer is good, but how you go about it is equally important. At this point you know how to call God through emergency phone calls. If you call the right number of God, you will get quick answer. This is the reason you hold the book in your hand.

Emergency phone calls of God are spiritual wine to life. It refreshes you and makes you proud of God. He shall be your strength every morning and your salvation in time of distress. In respond to your call, and at the thunder of his voice enemies will flee, when you look around enemies will scatter.

When you apply this book, God will give you grace to recognize opportunities around you and will not let them waste. There is no one who cannot be great if he/she uses time and opportunity right. You may lose them in the past, God shall restore them all. There is every reason to have the book in your hand. God is willing and ready to accept you for whom you are.

One thing you should know is, God is a secret keeper. This is the reason you run to him. He is with deep information you need to grow. To get this, you need right key to open door that answers challenges of life. It is when you have access to information and apply them you will be termed uncommon among equals and have uncommon success.

The time is now, the day is today and the year is this year, to apply right phone calls of God and shine. Failure is not written on your face. You are created excellence per see. Brethren, you are great, and great indeed. This book is for you. Pick it.

God bless you as you read on.

GOOD NEWS!!!

My audiobook is now available, to get one visit **audible**.

If you are reading from my paperback visit **acx.com** and search **"Tella Olayeri."**

Brethren, to be loaded and reloaded visit: *amazon.com/author/tellaolayeri* for a full spiritual sojourn for my books.

Thanks.

PREVIOUS PUBLICATIONS OF THE AUTHOR

Before we proceed, I'd like to say thank you for downloading this book. I believe the information in it will bless your life greatly. Please find below other books that God has empowered me write. They are meant to be a blessing to your life and family

1. .100% CONFESSIONS and PROPHECIES to Locate Helpers and helpers to locate you
2. 1000 Prayer Points for Children Breakthrough
3. 1010 (One Thousand and Ten) DREAMS and Interpretations
4. 2000 Dangerous Prayer for First Born
5. 365 DREAMS and INTERPRETATIONS
6. 430 Prayers to Cancel Bad Dreams and Overcome Witchcraft Powers part one (DREAMS AND YOU Book 1)
7. 430 Prayers to Claim Good Dreams and Overcome Witchcraft Powers part two (DREAMS AND YOU Book 2)
8. 630 Acidic Prayers: With Missile Prayer for Speedy Breakthrough, Healing and Deliverance
9. 650 DREAMS AND INTERPRETATIONS

94. Warfare Prayer Against Satanic Dream

See all at: amazon.com/author/tellaolayeri

Table of Contents

FREE BOOKS

We must not fold arms in the midst of battle. The life is battle itself. We need to pray and cancel decisions of darkness against us. We are born to win not to lose. Many times we lose out because we don't know how to pray or go about challenges we face.

Also, you must know how to claim and retain what God gives you, called destiny. You must not be robbed!

Brethren, your case is not close until you decide to close it. Don't give up, fight on in faith, you are born to win. Be violent in prayer. The degree of your violence in prayer determines the victory that awaits you. It is time you count spoils not loss, triumph not defeat.

I have some free books for you to put fire to your prayer zeal. Pick them and inform others. Try and share your experience with five to ten people. You may be the one God sent. Don't leave them outside prayer war room.

Be your brother/sister keeper. Good-luck

Click Here to Download

CHAPTER ONE

IF YOU FIND THE WORLD GROWING SMALL AND YOU GREAT...CALL PSALM 19

The world can only grow small and you great when you place total focus on God and treat the world small. The principle of primary and secondary come to play; the Lord or heaven is taken as primary while the world is termed secondary. Abraham practiced faith. Abraham surrendered his one and only son, at God's command. Eventually, the boy was saved, the family later became stars in number; out of it and in the fullness of time, appear Jesus Christ.

Sacrifice is the major tool you apply before you can surrender all. When you surrender all and accept poverty, God shall send you wealth. When you renounce a rich field of service, he sends you a richer one you never dreamt of. When you give up all your cherished hopes and die unto self, he sends you life more abundant with joy.

Your race is like of an eagle, that soars alone. No matter the situation be filled with courage. Eagle is a bird of courage. You cannot detain the eagle in the forest. When the eagle spreads its lofty wings, and with its eyes far into sky, it will soar away to its ancestral halls of rock. The soul of man, in its eagle soaring, will rest with nothing short of the Rock of Ages. Your ancestral hall is the hall of heaven.

Arise oh woman, arise oh man; the clock of the centuries points to the eleventh hour. God is looking for a man, or a woman, whose heart will be always set on him, and who will trust him for all he desires to do. God is eager to work more mightily now than he ever has through any soul.

God is set for men and women ready to do his work. God is waiting for one, who will be more fully devoted to him than any who have ever lived, who will be willing to be nothing that Christ may be all. God is looking for one who will grasp God's own purpose, do his will and without hindering continue to let God do exploits.

Men and women who surrender totally to God's work and will are full with joy fulfilled. George Mueller the great man of God discovered this some years after he became born again.

In an address given to ministers and workers after his ninetieth birthday; George Mueller spoke thus of himself. "I was converted in November 1825, but I only came into the full surrender of the heart four years later, in July 1829. The love of money was gone, the love of place was gone, the love of position was gone, and the love of worldly pleasure and engagements was gone. God alone became my portion. I found my all in Him, I wanted nothing else. And by the grace of God He has remained, and has made me a happy man, an exceedingly happy man, and it led me to care only about the things of God.

I ask affectionately, my beloved brethren, have you fully surrendered the heart to God, or is there this thing or that thing with which you are taken up irrespective of God? I need a little of the scriptures before, but preferred other books, but since that time the revelation He has made of Himself has become unspeakably blessed to me, and I can say from my heart, God is an infinitely lovely Being. Oh, be not satisfied I until in your own inmost soul you can say, God is an infinitely lovely being!"

In the life of George Mueller, the world grew smaller on the day he discovered to surrender all to God. For Four Years, despite being born again, he still love the affairs of the world. I pray this day;

God shall make you an extra ordinary Christian. You can't do it alone; you need God's blessing in prayer and supplications. Our great Helper in prayer is the Lord Jesus Christ, our Advocate with the Father, our Great High Priest, who's Chief Ministry for us these centuries has been intercession and prayer. He it is who takes our impact petition from our hands, cleanses them from their defects, corrects their faults and then claim answer from His Father on His own account and righteousness. He didn't do this alone but cleanse us from spiritual pollution, spiritual decadence and faults. If He does all these; we shouldn't give up along the line but embrace His support for us. He has gone in for us into the inner chamber and already holds up our names upon the palms of His hand; and the messenger, which is to bring you your blessing, is now on his way, and the spirit is only waiting your trust to whisper in your heart the echo of the answer from the throne, "It is done".

Alas, brethren, allow the world to grow small, and smaller; and yourself great and greater before the Lord. I pray you shall excel in the pursuit. Amen.

PRAYER POINTS

1. Spirit to focus on God and be great in life be my portion in the name of Jesus.

2. O Lord, give me life more abundant with joy in the name of Jesus.

3. O Lord, empower me to soar like eagle, in the name of Jesus.

4. O Lord, make me surrender all to serve you in the name of Jesus.

5. Courage and wisdom from above, fill my heart in the name of Jesus.

6. Every chain of darkness assign to detain me in one spot, break in the name of Jesus.

7. I shall abide in the Rock of Ages for protection and guidance in the name of Jesus.

8. Lord Jesus, use me to do exploit in the name of Jesus.

9. O Lord, in vision and in dream give me picture of who I am.

10. O Lord, let the love of money leave me to serve you in the name of Jesus.

11. O Lord, let the love of my home leave me to serve you in the name of Jesus.

12. O Lord, let the love of my position leave me to serve you in the name of Jesus.

13. O Lord, let the love of worldly pleasure and engagement leave me to serve you in the name of Jesus.

14. Lord Jesus, operate my heart, deposit heavenly message in it by your power.

15. As I surrender all to you O Lord, let the world grow smaller in eyes in the name of Jesus.

16. Lord Jesus, be my help in prayer.

17. Lord Jesus, be my advocate with God the Father.

18. Lord Jesus, be my Great High Priest, and tutor me in the word.
19. Lord Jesus, take my petition to God for quick answer.
20. Lord Jesus, cleanse my petition from defects, claim answer from God on my behalf.
21. Lord Jesus, do every correction needed in my petition as you table it before God so that I can be great in life.
22. Lord Jesus, defend my cause in the inner chamber of God.
23. Lord Jesus, write my name in the palms of your hand and remember me.
24. Things of the world shall not choke my chances to make heaven in the name of Jesus.
25. Every evil register that contains my name, catch fire and roast to ashes in the name of Jesus.
26. Every roaring lion assign to cage my faith die in the name of Jesus.

27. Every altar of darkness working against my destiny, catch fire and roast to ashes in the name of Jesus.

28. Powers that boast, that I will move from frying pan to fire shall woefully fail in the name of Jesus.

29. Destiny quenchers around me quit my life by fire in the name of Jesus.

30. O Lord, let me abide in your grace in the name of Jesus.

31. O Lord, let your angel ascend and descend for my sake in the name of Jesus.

32. Life in the valley, your time is up, die in the name of Jesus.

33. Lord Jesus, be my life partner till I make heaven.

CHAPTER TWO

FOR PAUL'S SECRET TO HAPPINESS…CALL COLOSSIANS 3:12-17

The vision of paradise by Paul is a great instrument that gave him joy even in the face of persecution. He said**, "Therefore I take pleasure in infirmities, in reproaches, in necessities, in persecutions, in distresses for Christ's sake: for when I am weak, then am I strong"**. 2 Corinthians 12:10.

The question is how can one have pleasure in negatives, such as infirmities, reproaches, persecutions, distress, oppositions etc. if something concrete and positive won't come out of it? The happiness and joy of Paul center on what he believed shall be soonest.

He is literally saying, "I take pleasure in being without strength, in insults, in being pinched, in being chased about, in being cooped up in a corner for Christ's sake, for when I am without strength then I am dynamite". Paul's source of strength is divine all-sufficient. This is a situation that demand emergency, but then, we choose to pleasantly love it. It is a stage in life we stop asking for sympathy because of our hard situation or bad treatment, for we will recognize these things as the very condition of our blessings.

There is joy in affliction. There is joy in thorns and in the cross. When Jesus was arrested, beaten, nailed on the cross and with thorns of crown, he knew exactly he was going to sit at the right hand of God. To his persecutors it was pains; to him joy. Joy must not rest only in roses but as well, thorns. This, George Matheson, the well-known blind preacher of Scotland said, "My God, I have never thanked Thee for my thorn, I have thanked Thee a thousand times for my roses, but not once for my thorn. I have been looking forward to a world where I shall get compensation for my cross; but I have never thought of my cross as itself a present glory.

Teach me the glory of my cross; teach me the value of my thorn, show me that I have climbed to thee by the path of pain. Show me that my tears have made my rainbows."

Paul's secret to happiness is ability to forge ahead in the midst of persecution. The laments of the sufferer are sign of fellowship with God. Storm of life trains the body for greatness. In the midst of storm, God withdraws his child to higher altitudes of fellowship, that he may near God, speaking face to face, and bear the message to his fellows at the mountain foot. Where the forty days wasted that Moses spent on the mount or period spent at Horeb by Elijah, or the years spent in Arabia by Paul?

Friendship is one major secret to Paul's happiness. He said to the Thessalonians, **"We loved you so much that we delighted to share with you not only the gospel of God but our lives as well, because you had become so dear to us"** 1 Thessalonians 2:8. Paul's joy in Thessalonica was not just the preaching of the gospel but the friendships he had. He preached the good news because he loved them.

Why did Paul want Timothy to visit him in prison? Did he merely want to receive the books and his winter coat? No, he wanted to see Timothy just for the joy of being with him, as a friend and 'son'.

The secret of happiness rests with God. Most times we relate our happiness to flesh, but full happiness is spiritual happiness. Flesh happiness relates to wealth of the world. Many believe once you are rich, you will be happy. This is ironically wrong. Wealth doesn't equate happiness, but only a fragment of happiness. You can be wealthy but sad. A wealthy person can be bed-ridden. A wealthy person may lose his jewel wife at prime age. This will destroy trace of happiness in him. A young boy/girl may have first class in the university, this is happiness to the family at large, but if the same person run mad a day after graduation, happiness disappears.

Happiness is therefore relative. But secret of happiness knows Christ. In a gathering of youth, two boys were made to stand up, to speak on happiness. The first one belongs to the world. He said my time of happiness is when I have fine babes around me, and or take beer and smoke. Everyone in the gathering knew him for this, so it is no news.

The second brother who happens to be in Christ stood and said, my moment of joy is having Christ in me and knowing that if the trumpet sounds today I shall ascend with Christ. This statement sound foolish to the ears of those who don't know Christ, but this brother knew what is good.

The secret of happiness rests with Christ. When Christ dwell in you, least shall you think of things of the world. To be in Christ doesn't mean one should be poor. Poverty is said, is a disease. No one pray to be poor in other to inherit the kingdom of God. If you die with your talent untapped, you will be questioned in heaven, for not allowing others to tap from your 'wealth'.

Happiness is a state of well-being and contentment. With happiness comes gladness. Psalm 4:7 says **"Thou hast put gladness in my heart, more than in the time that their corn and their wine increased"**. Thus, increase in wine cannot be compared to heavenly joy or happiness. Heavenly joy or joy that originates from God is close to Holy Spirit. The book of Acts of Apostles 13:52 says, **"And the disciples were filled with joy and with the Holy Spirit"**. Secret of happiness is akin to Holy Spirit to dwell in you. When it dwells in you fruit of the spirit; which is love, joy, peace, longsuffering, gentleness and faith shall find place in your life.

PRAYER POINTS

1. My source of happiness shall not be polluted by enemies in the name of Jesus.

2. O Lord, give me heavenly vision that erase doubts in my mind.

3. By the power of the living God, infirmities shall not take heavenly focus from me in the name of Jesus.

4. Every reproach I undergo shall not bring sorrow to my life, in the name of Jesus.

5. Persecution shall not diminish my joy in the name of Jesus.

6. Necessities of life shall not make me deny Jesus in the name of Jesus.

7. O Lord, give me heavenly strength to withstand all situations, in the name of Jesus.

8. Every opposition against my joy, scatter in the name of Jesus.

9. O Lord, turn me to dynamite in the hands of enemies in the name of Jesus.

10. Every arrow of affliction fired against me to miss heaven backfire in the name of Jesus.

11. Every dark thorn assign to choke my faith catch fire and roast to ashes in the name of Jesus.

12. The cross I will carry shall not be heavy than me to carry in the name of Jesus.

13. Affliction that opens heavens shall not swallow me in the name of Jesus.

14. Joy in affliction locate me by fire in the name of Jesus.

15. Joy in thorns, locate me by fire in the name of Jesus.

16. Joy in the cross, locate me by fire in the name of Jesus.

17. Every pain enemy design for me be converted to joy in the name of Jesus.

18. Every crown of sorrow enemy design for me shall be crown of glory for me in heaven in the name of Jesus.

19. My crown bring me glory in the name of Jesus.

20. O Lord, teach me the glory of my cross, so that my happiness will abound in the name of Jesus.

21. O Lord, teach me the value of my thorn, so that I will have strength to bear situations.

22. O Lord, let my tears form rainbows of hope and joy to propel my life in the name of Jesus.

23. My lament shall not be in vain, but marry me to Jesus in the name of Jesus.

24. Storms of life, train my body for greatness in the name of Jesus.

25. My days of fasting and prayer shall not be a waste in the name of Jesus.

26. O Lord, give me friends that will not lead me to hell fire in the name of Jesus.

27. O Lord, let spiritual happiness in me swallow flesh happiness in the name of Jesus.

28. Thou wealth of the world, you will not make me backslide in the name of Jesus.

29. Root of sadness in my life, dry up in the name of Jesus.

30. Heavenly wisdom enter my life and dwell in me in the name of Jesus.

31. Holy Spirit, fill my heart in the name of Jesus.

32. My name, be found in the register of heaven in the name of Jesus.

CHAPTER THREE

FOR UNDERSTANDING CHRISTIANITY...CALL CORINTHIANS 5:15-19

Christian race is full of mystery. Our spiritual conflicts are among our choicest blessings, and our great adversary is used to train us for her ultimate defeat. So temptation victoriously met doubles pure spiritual strength and equipment. When equipped with the word, with prayer and fasting, wisdom and knowledge, it will be possible to defeat enemy, capture him and make him fight in our ranks. He will dislodge his old camps, making them bow before you, seeing yourself flying on their shoulders in the like of what prophet Isaiah said of Israelites flying on the shoulders of the Philistines, the arch enemy of Israel. Isaiah 11:14. In emergency God do wonders.

In the midst of emergency you need patience to sail through. Patience play vital role in the life of

Christians. Most of us get anxious and worn out in times of difficulties. We allow songs of praise cease in our mouth. We would have been victorious if we had only waited first to see the unfolding of his plans, we should never have found ourselves landed in redundancy or retrace our steps with so many tears of shame.

Elijah did not lose hope or impatient as he watched the brook dry up. Week after week, with sound and steadfast spirit, he watched the dwindling brook, often tempted to stagger through unbelief, but refusing to allow the situation come between him and God. The brook was suddenly overtaken by silver thread at the foot of the largest pool around. The brook shrank fast, the birds fled; the wild creatures of field and forest come no more to drink. The brook dried. Only then to his patient and unwavering spirit, "The word of the Lord come saying, "Arise get thee to Zarephath". The patience of Elijah work wonders. He is yet to perfect further miracle even before he look to heaven and call down rain years later at Mount Carmel.

Is there difficulty in your way? This is a question most Christians fail to understand or answer in the course of journey. In our Christian race, many voices urge this course or the other. At times, we miss it all not knowing which step to take. You should as a Christian study circumstances and build value of secret fellowship with God. Go to God with your question; get direction from the light of his smile or the cloud of his refusal.

Be Christ-like, in everything you do. God is preparing his heroes, and when opportunity comes, he can fit them into their place in a moment, and the world will wonder where they came from.

In the midst of emergency, take heart! Our Lord Jesus goeth before thee. Whatever awaits us is encountered first by him. With eyes of faith, you can see his majestic presence in front, and when that cannot be seen it is dangerous to move forward. Your march is well taken care of by him. He would not allow you take a step too dangerous for you, too difficult for your feet or too trying for your strength.

Are you scared of marching forward? Don't fear Jesus is down in front. He is in every tomorrow. He is in the tomorrows. It is tomorrow that fills men with dread. Jesus is there already. All the tomorrows of our life have to pass him before they can get to us. Who is this Jesus? He is power for each moment of weakness. He is the hope for each moment of pain. He is the comfort for every sorrow, the sunshine and joy after rain.

Do you think you are cheated in the rank and file of the church or in your organization? Let's take the church as an example. If your place in God's ranks is a hidden and secluded one, beloved, do not murmur, do not complain, do not seek to get out of God's will, if he has placed you there.

Just where you think you are useless, God placed you there for a purpose. Work loyalty with believe he has chosen you for it. Guard your armour for his work.

The day will come when Jesus will give rewards, and he makes no mistakes, although some people may wonder how you come to merit such a reward, as they had never heard of you before. It is God's doing. He is a God that never sleeps. He apportions you with merit. Lift up your eyes unto the hills and go forward by fire, there is no other way.

The weapon you need most to build sound relationship with God is prayer. Heaven is not far from those who tarry on the mount with their Lord.

With meditation and prayer heavenly gates open. Our savior, Lord Jesus, laid example for quiet converse with his disciples, once on the peak of Hermon, but often on the sacred slope of Olivet. Every Christian should have his Olivet to address issues even in emergency. We need heart fellowship with God.

Your relationship with our father in heaven empowers you to command the day, command the night and year as well. It is high time as Christians to get back to visions, peep into heaven, conscious of the higher glory and the larger life, hold fast to Christ, keep altar on fire, so that it doesn't be a mere stone, unblessed by heaven! Therefore build your Olivet and command the day.

Daniel needed to have an Olivet in his chamber amid Babylon's roar and idolatries.

Joshua used command upon the heavenly when in the supreme moment of triumph. He lifted his spear toward the settling sun, and cries, "Sun, stand thou still"

Elijah used command when he shut the heavens for three years and six months, and again opened them

Peter found his Olivet in the "upper room" at Wittenberg, which is still held sacred.

Martin Luther used command when kneeling by the drying Melanchthon; he forbade death to take his prey.

It is high time we turn emergency to victory and suffocate power of fear that may dare us from moving forward. As we understand Christianity more this way, we shall forge ahead and be champion.

God bless, as you pray along.

PRAYER POINTS

1. Lord Jesus, empower me to command the day, every day.

2. Lord Jesus, empower me to command the year by your power.

3. O Lord, give me vision to see heaven in the name of Jesus.

4. I hold to Christ and shall not fail, in the name of Jesus.

5. My altar of prayer, receive fire in the name of Jesus.

6. O Lord, turn my emergency to victory in the name of Jesus.

7. I lift up my eyes unto the hill and move forward by fire in the name of Jesus.

8. Lord Jesus, gird my armour for your work.

9. Lord Jesus, do not pass me by, give me my reward at the right time.

10. Lord Jesus, build my soul for prayer to fight and win battle of life.

11. Thou gate of heaven open and favour me in the name of Jesus.

12. Lord Jesus, lead and take me to the mountain of prayer.

13. Spirit of murmur in my life, die in the name of Jesus.

14. I will not be useless in this generation or in heaven in the name of Jesus.

15. Spirit of impatience in my life die in the name of Jesus.

16. O Lord, occupy my tomorrow before it unfolds, in the name of Jesus.

17. Every dread that fills my tomorrow expire in the name of Jesus.

18. Lord Jesus, be the power of every moment of weakness in the name of Jesus.

19. Lord Jesus, be my hope for each moment of pain in my life.

20. Lord Jesus, be my comforter in every moment of sorrow I experience in the name of Jesus.

21. Lord Jesus be the sunshine and joy after rain in my life.

22. Wasters of life shall not waste me in the name of Jesus.

23. Every waster assign to waste me, be wasted in the name of Jesus.

24. Destiny swallower assign to wreck my destiny die in the name of Jesus.

25. Every gang up against me in the house of God, scatter in the name of Jesus.

26. Every gang up against me in my place of work, scatter in the name of Jesus.

27. Every gang up against me in my career, scatter in the name of Jesus.

28. Every gang up against me in my in-law's house scatter in the name of Jesus.

29. O Lord, give me breakthrough that will surprise everyone in the name of Jesus.

30. I fly on the shoulder of enemy and shine in the name of Jesus.

31. Every adversary fashion against my life, die in the name of Jesus.

32. O Lord, fill me with wisdom and knowledge to handle every situation of life.

33. Lord Jesus, make people wonder of the reward you gave me.

CHAPTER FOUR

FOR A GREAT INVENTION AND OPPORTUNITY…CALL ISAIAH 55

Greatness abound in us, the only limit is in us. Our asking, our thinking, our prayers are too small, our expectations are too limited. He is trying to lift us up to a higher height, and lure us on to a mightier expectation and appropriation. There is no limit to what we may ask and expect of our glorious El-Shadai.

It is high time we call on our amiable God. He is the God of boundless resources. He is extremely generous. He is abundantly able, able with an infinite surplus of resources. He promised Abraham of greatness and it came to pass. With faith Abraham did not stagger at the promise, but stood straight up unbinding until he received. Instead of growing weak he waxed strong in the faith and grew more robust.

We cry out early to God as if it is emergency, but it is time we are prepared for exploits. Little barriers at times look great in our sight. We want to achieve in the face of roses, this cannot be. Our Lord Jesus, never complain when arrested, he should be nailed to the cross afterward. Many want the glory without the cross, the shinning without the burning, but crucifixion comes before coronation. I pray, your cry to God at emergency time shall explode you to great exploits.

In order to experience great invention in life, you may have passed through many tribulations, researches, trials, toils, headaches, troubles, persecution or outright antagonism. In such condition, one may experience situations that call for emergency. You need light of hope to usher you forward. But then, shining is always costly. Light must be, before a person or place shines.

Light comes only at the cost of that which produces it.

The negatives and opportunities around you trigger your heart to fulfillment. These are what will lit the light of invention and opportunity in you. It is said, an unlit candle does not shine. Burning must come before shining. We cannot be of great use to others without cost to ourselves. Burning suggests suffering, which we often classify as emergency period.

In time of emergency, you may be surrounded with golden opportunities without knowing. Sometimes diamonds are done up in rough packages, so that their value cannot be seen. When the tabernacle was built in the wilderness there was nothing rich in its outward covering and rough badger skin gave no hint of the valuable things which it contained. Hence you should pray to God for inner eyes to discover and know what he has in stock for you.

God may send you some costly packages. Do not worry if they are done up in rough wrappings. You may be sure there are treasures of love, kindness and wisdom, great inventions and opportunities hidden within. If we take what he send, and trust him for the goodness in it, even in the dark, we shall learn the secrets of greatness. Christ is the master of every circumstance shaping you into a vessel of beauty and honour.

God will not show you the chart of all his purpose concerning you. He will show you only into a way where, if you go cheerfully and trustfully forward, he will show you on still further. Pray to realize when you are at door of entrance, open it and enter, and you will find river of opportunity broader and deeper than anything you may imagine in your sunniest dreams.

It is time you discover yourself. Pray for great vision of excellence. Climb to the treasure house of blessing on the ladder made of divine promises. Cry out loud and possess David's key that opens the door to the riches of God's grace and favour

Invention doesn't mean work alone, you rest to reload your strength. Create Sunday in your working days; create Sunday hours in your working hours as well. Sundays are meant for rest. Yet no time is profitably spent than that which is set apart for quiet musing, for talking with God, for looking up to heaven. "Reverie" it has been said, "is the Sunday of the mind"
Brethren, let us often give our mind a "Sunday" in which it will do no manner of work but simply lie still, and look upward for dews of blessings of heaven.

Let there be intervals when we shall do nothing, think nothing, plan nothing, but just lay ourselves on the green lap of nature and "rest a while" as did Isaac.

"And Isaac went out to mediate in the field at the eventide" Genesis 24:63. Time so spent is not lost time rather, it makes heart with new joy and hope.

PRAYER POINTS

1. O God arise, and let my star shine in the name of Jesus.
2. O God arise, empower me to discover opportunities around me.
3. Greatness that abound in me manifest in the name of Jesus.
4. Power to pray and discover self, fall upon me in the name of Jesus.
5. O Lord, enlarge my coast to the dismay of my enemy, in the name of Jesus.

6. O Lord, lift me to a higher height to accomplish my destiny in the name of Jesus.

7. Lord Jesus, lure me to a mightier expectation of fulfillment in the name of Jesus.

8. O Lord, with your boundless resources bless me abundantly in the name of Jesus.

9. O Lord, in your extreme generosity, do not count me out among those you will bless.

10. Every lack in me be converted to surplus by the power of Jesus.

11. O Lord, open my eyes to vision of greatness in the name of Jesus.

12. Every covenant with evil power break in the name of Jesus.

13. Lord Jesus, make covenant of prosperity with me to excel.

14. O Lord, build my faith to forge ahead in life.

15. Every limitation in me blocking my opportunity, expire in the name of Jesus.

16. I shall not grow weak but shall wax strong in faith to serve the Lord and prosper, in the name of Jesus.

17. O Lord, give me wisdom to exploit opportunities around me in the name of Jesus.

18. O Lord, you are abundantly able, turn little in me to BIG, in the name of Jesus.

19. Every barrier between me and breakthrough, scatter in the name of Jesus.

20. O Lord, give me power to carry the cross that bring roses, in the name of Jesus.

21. Every crucifixion I pass through lead to coronation in the name of Jesus.

22. O Lord, convert my trials to triumph in the name of Jesus.

23. O Lord, convert my failure to success in the name of Jesus.

24. O Lord, convert my defeat to victory in the name of Jesus.

25. O Lord, convert my poverty to prosperity in the name of Jesus.

26. O Lord, convert my scars to stars in the name of Jesus.

27. O Lord, convert my weakness to strength in the name of Jesus.

28. O Lord, convert my frustration to fulfillment in the name of Jesus.

29. Any power prolonging my stay in the wilderness of life, die in the name of Jesus.

30. Every terror of the night against my destiny, scatter in the name of Jesus.

31. I plant seed of breakthrough and fertilize it with blood of Jesus.

32. My leg carry me to my place of breakthrough in the name of Jesus.

33. My destiny, rest on pillar of breakthrough in the name of Jesus.

CHAPTER FIVE

FOR HOW TO GET ALONG WITH FELLOW MEN CALL…ROMANS 12

We try to understand fellow men, but God understand better. We look at face, dress and at times speech and attitude of people, but God searches the heart. He judges us according to our heart. He knows better and does better. With rumours, our minds are polluted against each other. God doesn't believe or act to rumour.

The rumour of Saul, who later became Paul, killer of Apostles, feared Ananias, but the same Saul (Paul) became good instrument in the hand of God. Ananias initially argued with the Lord as one to go and face the 'killer of Apostles, Saul, but thank God, he obeyed and became the one to anoint the greatest Apostle.

It is not often easy to get along with fellowmen. Yet, we are called to be God's ambassadors, His missionaries, the light of the world in a time of chaos and great darkness and unfriendliness from people. Yours is not an exception, to Jesus disciples Jerusalem was hostile to them. Samaria was their natural enemy.

Determination is one major factor that endear you get along or not with fellow men. In the face of discouragement you determine what to do. The soul of your heart should be deep with honest purpose. There was this story. When a Roman soldier was told by his guide that if he insisted on taking a certain journey it would probably be fatal, he answered, "It is necessary for me to go, it is necessary for me to live" This is determination. No matter what, he has taken decision.

The fact is, we are always afraid of trials and sorrow, only after miracles. If Joseph had not been

Egypt's prisoner, he never would have been Egypt's governor. The iron chain about his feet ushered in the golden chain about his neck. Joseph's dungeon is the road to Joseph's throne. Even the adversary becomes an auxiliary, and the things that seem to be against us turn out to be for the furtherance of our way.

You come across different persons with diverse characters on daily basis. Therefore, you need wisdom and heavenly process to carry you along. The best thing of life comes out of wounding. Wheat is crushed before its odours are set free. The ground must be broken with the sharp plough before it is ready to receive the seed. It is the broken heart that pleases God. The sweetest joys in life are the fruits of sorrow. Human nature needs suffering to fit in to being a blessing to the world.

Character differs, one need to endure to get along with fellow men and women. The one you mix with today may be quite different from the one you meet tomorrow. Abraham was long tried, but he was richly rewarded.

The Lord tried him delaying to fulfill his promise. Satan tried him by temptation; men tried him by jealousy, distrust and opposition. Sarah tried him by her talks. But he patiently endured both men and God. He never question God nor limit his power, or doubt his faithfulness, nor grieve his love, but he bowed to divine sovereignty, submitted to infinite wisdom, and was silent under delays, waiting the Lord's time. When you trust and rest on God to get along with men becomes easy, as he loads you with wisdom to handle issues.

Relationship with fellow men and women matters as we pass through this world. It affects daily life of whosoever you interact or do business with. There is a story of an old man who carried a little

Can of oil with him everywhere he went, and if he passed through a door that makes noise as a result of bad hinges, he poured a little oil on the hinges. If a gate was hard to open, he oiled the latch. And thus he passed through life lubricating all hard places and making it easier for those who came after him. People called him eccentric, odd, unusual fellow etc. but the old man never mind the talks of people, went steadily on refilling his Can of oil when it became empty, and oiled hard places he found.

There are many lives that need support as they live day by day. Nothing goes right with them. They need lubricating with the oil gladden, gentleness, or thoughtfulness. Have you your own Can of oil with you? Be ready with your oil of helpfulness in the early morning to the one nearest to you. It may lubricate the whole day for him. The oil of good cheer to the down hearted one. Brethren, speak the word of courage to the despairing. Note this, our lives touch others, but once perhaps, on the road of life, and then, afterwards, our ways, diverge, never to meet again.

PRAYER POINTS

1. O Lord, guide me in my daily activities in the name of Jesus.

2. O Lord, enable my heart with blood of Jesus.

3. I cleanse my heart with blood of Jesus.

4. Every fear that will make me lose what God ordain for me, die in the name of Jesus.

5. O Lord, make me your ambassador in the name of Jesus.

6. O Lord, make me your missionary in the name of Jesus.

7. O Lord, make me the light of the world in a time of chaos.

8. Every hostile environment against me be silenced in the name of Jesus.

9. Any environment that turns natural enemy to me, be overthrown be the power of Holy Ghost.

10. Determination to forge ahead with God's will for my life, possess me.

11. O Lord, convert my trials to triumph in the name of Jesus.

12. O Lord, give me wisdom to handle people I meet on daily basis.

13. O Lord, mold me to suit your need in the name of Jesus.

14. Every temptation on my way, be defeated by fire in the name of Jesus.

15. Every jealousy that will hinder me of breakthrough scatter in the name of Jesus.

16. Every opposition against me scatter in the name of Jesus.

17. I shall not doubt faithfulness of God upon my life, in the name of Jesus.

18. I shall not fail in the pursuit of good things of life.

19. My star arise and shine in the name of Jesus.

20. O Lord, give me merry heart to associate with others, in the name of Jesus.

21. Holy Spirit, load me with fire of understanding.

22. My words, move mountain wherever I go, in the name of Jesus.

23. Lord Jesus, make me complete in you by fire.

24. I decree, anyone I come across shall speak good of me.

25. Every wall between me and my helper, collapse in the name of Jesus.

26. I abide in the strong tower of the Almighty, in the name of Jesus.

27. No weapon fashion against me shall prosper in the name of Jesus.

28. Enemy shall not have dominion over my life, in the name of Jesus.

29. Owner of evil load carry your load in the name of Jesus.

30. O Lord, give me Can of oil to lubricate life of people I come across.

31. O Lord, fill my mouth with word of courage in the name of Jesus.

32. Peace of God, reign in my life, in the name of Jesus.

33. Thou power of darkness vacate my life in the name of Jesus.

CHAPTER SIX

FOR DEALING WITH FEAR...CALL PSALM 34:7

Shakespeare wrote, cowards die many times before their death. The ten spies saw giants, but Caleb and Joshua saw God! Fear makes us see giants taller than us. Giants stand for great difficulties, occupying everywhere. They are in our family, in churches, in our social life, in the hearts, and we must overcome them or they will eat us up. Here, we need to apply faith of superiority and strength. We must look at giants as bread for us, or else, they may consume us in our path.

Fear is one instrument Satan use as weapon. He knows when you are filled with fear; it will be hard to take right decision. Your heart disorganizes and you are not in form. He shall be able to cajole you to submission and deal with you. Fear is not what we should allow to operate in our life.

It is good to phone God, when fear appears in the corridor of our life, or is hard on us. Esther must have initially think how unlucky to be the one to approach the king, as the step can lead to sudden death. Alas, she chased spirit of fear out of her and headed to the king saying, "If I perish, I perish" This is always the situation in time of emergency. But God had excellence of Moddecai in mind, and fall of Haman to pass. When Esther nullifies fear in her mind, doors of opportunities appeared.

With boldness, facts and wisdom, giants are defeated and eliminated. In the spirit giants are bold, stubborn, rude, powerful and wicked. You must therefore equip yourself before you can subdue them. Therefore, when you see a giant, remember the road you must travel to come up; to his side is not where wildflowers ever bloom; but a steep, rocky, narrow pathway where the blasts of the hell will almost blow you off your feet; where the sharp rock cut the flesh, where thorns scratch the body, and the venomous beasts hiss on every side.

What an awful experience when one is to face or defeat a giant. Do you experience spiritual blow, scratch or cuts that made you conclude, "This is emergency". Mind you, every pathway you come across in emergency is full of sorrow and joy, of suffering and healing balm, of tears and smiles, of trials and victories, of conflicts and triumphs, of hardships and perils.

You know it today. Therefore, don't shrink back from the ordeal of fierce storm of trials; rather go in, meet the giant and defeat it! God is there to meet you in the centre of all your trials and to whisper his secrets which will make you come forth with a shining face.

As long as there is fear in our hearts, we will never understand what God is saying. It took Jacob many years to understand, but we do not need such a long time. Jesus has conquered our fears.

In the walk of life claim victory. There is no enemy in your Christian work, which was not included in your saviour's conquests. Touch them, they will flee before you. Even mere seeing you makes them shiver. It is written, **"You will not fear the terror of night, nor the arrows that fly by day, nor the pestilence that stalks in the darkness, nor the plague that destroys at midday"** Psalm 91:5-6

Why fear temptation and trials? The Bible says, **"If the cloud be full of rain, they empty themselves upon the earth"** Ecclesiastes 11:3. Why then do we dread clouds which now darken our sky; when rain of blessings shall soon empty up on us? True for a while they hide the sun. It is at this point we entertain fear, believing it is emergency period. We fear trials, we fear failure. This is the problem with human being. We quickly forget the sun is not quenched; it will be out before long. Meanwhile those black clouds are filled with rain, and the blacker they are, the more likely they will yield plentiful showers of favour and blessings.

Brethren, fear not, how can we have rain without clouds? Our troubles have always brought us blessings, and they always will. They are the dark chariots of bright grace and mercy. These clouds will empty themselves very soon, and every vegetation will be gladdened for the shower of blessings this day in the name of Jesus.

Why do you entertain fear in the presence of the Lord? Why look at the world instead of Jesus? The fact is what people regard as the end of life is the very preparation for coronation. Where your death seems to be, our Saviour Lord Jesus awaits you. Where the end of hope is, there is the brightest beginning of fruition. Where the darkness is thickest, there the bright beaming light that never set about to emerge. Your joy is made better if there be sorrow in the midst of them.

Fear not, be strong and courageous. The Lord is with you thou man, thou woman of mighty valour. You are mighty because you are with the mightiest. Learn the habit to claim victory. Therefore, claim victory, I say, claim victory all the time. Whenever your enemies close in upon you, claim victory! Whenever heart and flesh fail, look up and claim victory. You have a share in that triumph which Jesus won. Remember that you were in him when he won it. You are one of the conquering legions of the Lord; therefore claim your share in the Saviour's victory. Let fear depart in your life. You are a winner!

PRAYER POINTS

1. Every giant causing fear in my life, die in the name of Jesus.

2. Every giant that stands between me and breakthrough die in the name of Jesus.

3. Every giant chasing helpers away from me die in the name of Jesus.

4. Every giant that boast I shall not make it, you are not my God, die in the name of Jesus.

5. Every giant assign to put evil load on my head, carry your evil load and die in the name of Jesus.

6. Every giant that occupy my seat of glory, I unseat you in the name of Jesus.

7. Every giant holding my cup of breakthrough release it and die in the name of Jesus.

8. Every weapon of darkness fashion against me backfire in the name of Jesus.

9. Every fear that grips my heart, expire in the name of Jesus.

10. Fear of the unknown in my heart, your time is up, die in the name of Jesus.

11. O Lord, give me boldness to chase fear out of me.

12. Wisdom to handle light and hard situation fill my heart in the name of Jesus.

13. Thou giant holding me to ransom, you are rude, die in the name of Jesus.

14. Every serpent and scorpion on my way, I match you to death in the name of Jesus.

15. Healing balm of God, heal my heart in the name of Jesus

16. Every failure as a result of fear, be converted to success in the name of Jesus.

17. Every hardship caused by fear, come to an end in the name of Jesus.

18. I walk to the gate of giant and defeat him/her in the name of Jesus.

19. Every terror of the night, die in the name of Jesus.

20. Every arrow that fly by day, backfire in the name of Jesus.

21. Every pestilence that stalks in the darkness, die in the name of Jesus.

22. Every plague that destroy at midday, die in the name of Jesus.

23. Thou cloud in the sky be converted to rain of blessing upon my life in the name of Jesus.

24. O Lord, turn my trial to triumph, in the name of Jesus.

25. Workers of iniquity assign against my life, die in the name of Jesus.

26. Every thick darkness in my life be converted to bright light in the name of Jesus.

27. Every curse pronounced against me backfire in the name of Jesus.

28. Anointing that break the yoke, fall upon me in the name of Jesus.

29. Every emptiness in my life, expire in the name of Jesus.

30. Rulers of darkness against my life die in the name of Jesus.

31. I claim victory over my enemy in the name of Jesus.

32. O Lord, let your grace and mercy be upon me today in the name of Jesus.

33. Praise the Lord, my Lord Jesus has conquered my fear.

CHAPTER SEVEN

FOR SECURITY…CALL PSALM 121:3

We need security one way or the other. It is the entire responsibility of God. There is none beside him to help. The book of 2 Chronicles 14:11 says, **"Lord, there is none beside thee to help"** This reminds us, human efforts are immaterial at times, but God's will and support. No matter enormous of odds against you, the Lord is able to secure you from danger. There may be a million gang up against you, it shall scatter. Every arm against you shall fail, when you look unto God for security.

The fact remains, devil will not take a break and leave us alone, or that we will not make mistakes. The assurance is, if God is by our side, we shall not be the first, or be the last to stumble or fall on earthly or heavenly race. Our tracts are full of long lineage of people that stumbled, made mistakes or lied. Yet God in his infinite mercy make us to stand at the end of the day.

Security lies with God; it is of the Lord's mercy that we are not consumed. Through all challenges, he stands by us. Our Lord makes us stand through whatever it is thrown at us. The Lord who delivers us in the seventh shall deliver us in all. **"From six calamities he will rescue you; in seven no harm will befall you."** Job 5:19

Our God is Omniscience. He is a God of miracles. He can reverse the gear of life from impending danger. He doesn't accept or tolerate wicked advancement of stubborn pursuers against his elect. Egypt paid dearly for it, when they rose against Israel. Not long after the death of first born sons of Egyptians, sorrow was added when their chariots and soldiers sank in the Red Sea as they pursed Israel in their march to the Promised Land. It was high tension and agony in Egypt on that day. Hence, I pronounce agony and regrets upon every stubborn pursuers of your life. Amen

Human life is threatened in various ways, through blackmail, direct threat, tribal pitfalls, hopelessness, unbelief, gang up, etc. But then, no matter what you pass through, don't give up, but rely on God and call his emergency phone number. The phone number is Psalm 121:3. He will not suffer thy foot to be moved; "He that keepeth thee will not slumber" as your feet takes you to places. God is there to direct your feet from the snares of the fowler. He is twenty four hours in charge, seven days alert, and 365 days in readiness to save you from all danger.

Always put God between you and the foes. When you do this, Celestial combatant shall fling themselves against the foes in your behalf. Both large and tiny armies against you shall be routed out. You will only wake up to gather spoils of the enemy. You hardly put much strength to overcome. It is God doing the battle for you. At last you shall experience security anywhere you go.

In the office insecurity shall fade away, and after the dust, comes promotion. In the pursuit of business and contracts, every obstacle, gang up and or promise and fail shall vanish. Amen. Those who gang up against you shall suddenly turn around to support you. By this, you shall not miss what belongs to you. Heavenly security shall secure your business for you. Do you experience marital insecurity? Heavenly angels shall guide and guard your marriage from wickedness of men and women. You shall experience joy in your marriage, and never shall it break. Amen.

Our God is a Jehovah of hosts, who can summon unexpected reinforcements at any time to save his people. What you should do, is to believe in him.

The Lord is there between you and your challenge. What baffles you shall flee and appear no more.

Are you confuse in the like of Asa King of Judah who shouted in the manner of , **"Lord, there is no one like you to help the powerless against the mighty"** 2 Chronicle 14:11. He faced threat of insecurity from his foes. The odds against Asa were enormous. There were a million men in arms against him, besides three hundred chariots seemed impossible to hold his own against vast multitude. There were no allies who would come to his help, his only hope, therefore was in God. He cried unto God, who turned insecurity to security and impossibility to possibility.

Brethren, I say again, put God between you and the foe. Doing this shall give opportunity to nullify every form of insecurity. In the face of defeat run to God, who can do all things? Asa did, and the celestial combatants flung themselves against the foe on Israel's behalf, and put the large host to rout, so that Israel had only to follow up and gather the spoil. Our God is Jehovah of hosts, who can summon unexpected reinforcements at any moment to aid his people. Believe the Lord Almighty is there between you and difficulty, and what baffles you shall flee, as clouds before the sun.

The Bible gives a number of passages to strengthen hope that God is with us. Read the following passages and build your faith

Isaiah 43:2b. **"When thou walkest through the fire, thou shalt not be burned, neither shall the flame kindle upon thee"**.

Daniel 3:25, 27. **"These men, upon whose bodies the fire had no power, nor was an hair of their head singed"**.

Job 5:19. **"He shall deliver thee in six troubles; ye in seven there shall no evil touch thee".**

Psalm 121:7. **"The Lord shall preserve thee from all evil".**

Luke 10:19. **"I give you power… nothing shall by any means hurt you".**

Exodus 23:22. **"I will be an enemy unto thine enemies".**

2 King 17:39. **"The Lord your God ye shall fear, and he shall deliver you out of the hand of all your enemies"**

2 Chronicles 32:8. **"With us is the Lord our God… to fight our battles".**

Psalm 18:16:17. **"He delivered me from my strong enemy... for they were too strong for me"**.

Psalm 97:10. **"He delivereth them out of the hand of the wicked"**

Psalm 138:7. **"Thou shalt stretch forth thine hand against the wrath of mine enemies, and thy right hand shall save me"**.

Isaiah 54:17. **"No weapon that is formed against thee shall prosper'**

Jeremiah 1:19. **"They shall fight against thee, but they shall not prevail... for I am with thee to deliver thee"**.

Psalm 91:7**. "A thousand shall fall at thy side, and ten thousand at thy right hand, but it shall not come nigh thee"**.

Luke 21:17, 18. **"Ye shall be hated of all nations... but there shall not one air of your head perish'**

PRAYER POINTS

1. Angels of God, guide me 24 hours every day in the name of Jesus.

2. O Lord, keep watch over me and let my enemies be helpless.

3. Shadow of God protect me from evil in the name of Jesus.

4. O Lord, deliver me from the hands of strong enemies.

5. O Lord, turn every impossibility in my life to possibility.

6. O heaven, favour me before men and God in the name of Jesus.

7. Every marine power fashion against me die in the name of Jesus.

8. Enemy may fight against me but they shall not prosper in the name of Jesus.

9. No weapon fashion against me shall prosper in the name of Jesus.

10. O Lord, cover me with your feathers, let me find refuge under your wings.

11. Enemies after me shall be like grass on the roof that withers before, it can grow.

12. As the mountains surround Jerusalem, so shall the Lord surround me, in the name of Jesus.

13. Every terror of the night against me die and rise no more in the name of Jesus.

14. O Lord, scatter every plague assign to destroy me, in the name of Jesus.

15. O Lord, punish the wicked after my life in the name of Jesus.

16. Angels of God, lift me in your hands, so that I strike no foot against a stone.

17. Whirlwind shall not consume me in the name of Jesus.

18. O Lord, you are my refuge and my fortress, let it be in the name of Jesus.

19. Every intimidation against me scatter in the name of Jesus.

20. Every dark lion assign against me die in the name of Jesus.

21. Every fowler's snare assign for me catch fire in the name of Jesus.

22. The sun will not harm me by day nor the moon by night.

23. Every arrow fired against me backfire in the name of Jesus.

24. Every pestilence that stalks in darkness against me die in the name of Jesus.

25. I will not die but live to proclaim the glory of the Lord, in the name of Jesus.

26. Every deadly pestilence after my life, die in the name of Jesus.

27. As from today, I shall tread upon serpents and scorpion unhurt in the name of Jesus.

28. O Lord, make my enemy footstool under my feet in the name of Jesus.

29. I am an anointed child of God, no harm shall befall me in the name of Jesus.

30. O Lord, give me long life to serve you.

31. O Lord, deliver me from evil and honour me in the name of Jesus.

32. I decree unto my life today, no disaster will come near my home in the name of Jesus.

33. I decree unto my life today, no harm shall come before me in the name of Jesus.

CHAPTER EIGHT

POWER FOR ASSURANCE…CALL MARK 8:35

It is crystal clear that the Holy Bible is the only 'Wise Old Book' that gives assurance to life and existence. It is like flower that never die, like the Easter Lilies! Holy poets are written for us to recite and to feed us with wisdom and knowledge. When down and out, or when you want to re-kindle fire of revival in you there are multiple verses of Psalms that can be turned to songs.

Natures are not left out. Trees that blossom are mentioned, birds of features of encouragement are brought to remembrance to give us hope. The sea and the sky speak volume of assurance. What more? We can say this:-Wise Old Book!, let me read again in your pages of firm assurance that to die is gain, and to know you leads to eternity. No book on earth can be compared to you. Your words are gateway to book of life.

Flowers! Easter Lilies! speak to me every time of the day. The words in you are always fresh to refresh the mind. Speak to me the same dear old lesson of immortality which you have been speaking to so many sorrowing souls for assurance that my God liveth.

Singers! break forth once more into songs of joy. The book of Psalms speaks volume of wonderful songs of assurance and dignity. My Holy Bible, I hold you tight to myself for spiritual digestion. Let me hear again the well-known resurrection Psalms of hope and assurance. Let songs of joy and assurance burst forth in me.

Poets!, recite to me your verses which repeat salvation to my soul. Poet that opens doors of wisdom. Poet that heals wounds. Poet of hope and joy that repeat in every line the gospel of eternal life. No poetry ever match you, oh my Holy Bible!

Tree and blossom and bird and sea and sky and wind whisper it, sound it afresh, echo it, and sound it loud to willing ears. Its message go wide and far. It is like holy earthquake! It sounds and drums assurance into every willing ear.

Let be told and retold and still retold until hope rises to full that Holy Bible gives full assurance and hope. Conviction therein is incomparable to any book. Even though going to our death, we go with triumphant mind, with serene and shining face.

I will lift up my eyes to God's eternal blue. I receive assurance that bitterness and sadness are gone in my life. My soul thrills to the caress of gladness. Failure disappears in my life. My destiny receives dews and showers of blessings. Every dark alarm is silenced. What more?

I shall experience marital bliss. My marriage shall not break. Whatever I lay hands upon shall prosper. Every gang up against me shall scatter. Joy shall flow continuously in me because I enjoy heavenly assurance.

Who shall I pick as friend in the crusade for assurance? I look left and right, front and back, it is Apostle Paul. Who said, in 2 Timothy 4:7-8 **"I have fought a good fight, I have finished my course, I have kept the faith: Henceforth, there is laid up for me a crown of righteousness, which the Lord, the righteous judge, shall give me at that date; and not to me only, but unto all them also that love his appearing"**

PRAYER POINTS

1. O Lord, build faith of assurance in my heart.
2. My knowledge of the world shall not be in vain in the name of Jesus.
3. My Bible, refresh my mind and build faith.
4. My soul, receive heavenly salvation in the name of Jesus.
5. My heaven open and favour me, in the name of Jesus.
6. My ears receive assurance of God for right direction.
7. My ears receive assurance of God so that my life will move forward.
8. I shall rise and shine, even to my last day on earth, in the name of Jesus.
9. Powers that distribute sadness, my life is not for you, die in the name of Jesus.
10. My heart, reject bitterness by fire, in the name of Jesus.
11. My soul, be filled with gladness and joy, in the name of Jesus.

12. Grip of failure in my life, loose your hold in the name of Jesus.

13. Every arrow of wickedness fired against me backfire in the name of Jesus.

14. Failure, disappear in my life in the name of Jesus.

15. O Lord, feed me with wisdom and knowledge in the name of Jesus.

16. My destiny, receive dews and showers of blessing in the name of Jesus.

17. Foundational problems hunting my destiny die in the name of Jesus.

18. Every covenant of sorrow, break in the name of Jesus.

19. My spirit shall not fail in my Christian race in the name of Jesus.

20. O Lord, let laughter break forth from my mouth, in the name of Jesus.

21. O Lord, prepare me as one of your heroes to fight, conquer and excel.

22. Whatever I lay hands on prosper, usher me to coast of prosperity.

23. Every gang up against me, scatter in the name of Jesus.

24. River of joy, flow into my life in the name of Jesus.

25. Every altar of darkness against me be dismantle in the name of Jesus.

26. Balm of Gilead, heal me from my head to toes in the name f Jesus.

27. Curses of local gods, break and be cancelled in the name of Jesus.

28. Satanic garment in my body, tear to pieces in the name of Jesus.

29. My prayer chase enemy away and destroy them in the name of Jesus.

30. My lost glory be restored today in the name of Jesus.

31. Lord Jesus, lay up for me crown of righteousness.

32. Lord Jesus, come to me, I pick you as friend in the crusade of assurance.

33. O Lord, honour me, energize me to fight good fight of assurance and accomplishment.

CHAPTER NINE

POWER FOR HEALING CALL…MATHEW 4:23-25

Where can one find divine healing? It is through the Almighty God. He is our INSIDE GOD. He is a Father, Son, and Holy Spirit, in the midst of me, just as the sun is in the center of the heavens. He is in the midst, at the center of my physical being. He is in the midst of my brain. He is in the Centre of my nerve. It is not only a living reality to me, but a reality growing deeper and richer, making me in every sense younger and fresher than ever. With divine healing is strength of God, doing full twice as much work, mental and physical, with less than half the effort than necessary. Your life, physical, mental and spiritual is like heavenly well, always overflowing. Your body, soul and spirit are redeemed, sanctified and healed. What more?

The living Christ passes moment by moment into our redeemed body, filling, energizing, and vitalizing it with the presence and power of his own personality, turning our own whole being into a "New heaven and New Earth". Divine healing is just divine life. It is the headship of Christ over the body. It is the union of our members with the very body of Christ and the in flowing life of Christ in our living members.

Healing bring radical change in corporate life. Inner spiritual healing is an eye opener. It makes us discover new delight in worship and belief. When the women with issue of blood got healed she danced as she never did before. She praised God as she never praise before. She was full of surprises, her heart gladdens. To experience divine healing may include ministering to the heart of God using simple songs to express our love to him, and plain objective language to exalt his name. As we do this, our hearts melt towards him and towards each other.

Inward healing attracts Holy Spirit. The gifts of the Spirit – prophecy, tongues, interpretation of tongues, words of knowledge etc. come to play. Inner healing brings deliverance, signs and wonders, and learning under the Holy Spirit. When Holy Spirit is in control, sins are exposed and confessed, while repentant tears are shed.

Social healing is paramount and needed. In the past most families tended to live their lives within the communities in which they were born. By residing close together they were available to help each other out with their individual crisis. These days families are easily and quickly uprooted and find themselves widely scattered, sometimes across the world.

Too many people today, when faced with serious difficultly have no familiar face to turn to. Marriages are falling apart, divorce rates are rising; one-parent families are on the increase – some from choice and some through tragedy. Their offspring are suffering. The human problems are compounded. The net result is an explosion in the number of hurting people in our society. This social disorder needs healing.

Our past can invade our present and affect our future. Emotions like anger or fear become attach to past traumatic experiences. An experience today presses some "Hot Button" within that makes heart bleed. A child sexually assaulted when small may have a distorted view of sex and a fear of close relationship as he or she becomes adult. From experience, women who were molested sexually as small children; don't like men close to them. This is an inappropriate reaction for an adult, but a reflex one that is uncontrolled.

Some people may be able to recollect a particular traumatic event that caused emotional damage. Whether general or specific everyone has some buried inner pain inflicted in early childhood, may be even from the womb. Deep inside each of us are primal needs for security, self-worth, and significance which have either never been met at all, or only insufficiently. Some babies have lacked adequate food, some have lacked a loving embrace, some have lacked parental bonding. Some have suffered cruelty and some have been left to cry for longer than was bearable.

Were you violated as a child? There are children who have endured the loss of one or even both parents; children who have experienced long stays in hospital, or have been 'evacuated' from parents and familiar home surroundings; some have been deeply wounded by perceived favours to rival siblings. Some children have been sexually violated by a relative, and some molested or sadistically beaten by a parent or school master.

The list of hurts inflicted deliberately or involuntarily by our fallen world is unending. Our future may depend on what we decide to do in the present with our past. The damaged emotions caused by past experience must be healed. We cannot change history, but the feelings surrounding it can be changed by Jesus who is able to transcend time and bring healing to the past. **Jesus Christ is the same yesterday and today and forever"** Hebrew 13:8

God knows best how to heal us. God knows everything about us. The Psalmist says, **"My frame was not hidden from you when I was made in the secret place. When I was woven together in the depths of the earth, your eyes saw my unformed body. All the days ordained**

for me were written in your book before one of them came to be" Psalm 139:15-16

Above all, we must know the authority we have in Jesus. In his name there is healing for our hurts. In his name there is authority over the kingdom of darkness. In his name there is power to break bondages that have enslaved us for years. In his name is loaded with divine healing.

There is hope in the Lord, only summon courage and believe.
The Bible says in:

Psalm 34:18. **"The Lord is nigh unto them that are of a broken heart"**

Exodus 15:26b. **"I am the Lord that healeth thee".**

Deuteronomy 7:15. **"The Lord will take away from thee all sickness".**

Psalm 103:3. **"He forgiveth all iniquities, healeth all thy diseases".**

Jeremiah 30:17a**. "For I will restore health unto thee, and will heal thee"**

Malachi: 4:2a. **"Sun of righteousness arise with healing in his wings".**

Mark 1:40, 41. **"Lord, if thou wilt…Jesus saith, I will, be thou clean".**

Act of Apostles 9:34a. **"Jesus Christ makes thee whole"**

Psalm 22:24. **"He hath not despised…affliction of the afflicted, neither hath he hid his face from him".**

Isaiah 53:5. **"He was wounded… with his stripes we are healed".**

Matthew 8:16, 17. **"He himself took our infirmities and bore our sickness"**

1 Peter 2:24. **"By whose stripes ye were healed".**

Jeremiah 32:27. **"I am the Lord…is there anything too hard for me"**

Matthew 19:26. **"With God all things are possible"**

2 King 20:5b. **"I have… seen thy tears, behold, I will heal thee"**

2 Chronicles 7:14. **"If my people humble themselves, and pray and turn from their wicked ways, then will I hear and heal".**

Psalm 91:10. **"There shall no evil befall thee, neither shall any plague come nigh thy dwelling"**

Mark 16:18a. **"If they drink any deadly thing, it shall not hurt them".**

Call God today in prayer, call his emergency phone number. Your call brings answer. You shall experience divine healing from your head to the sole of your feet. Bruises and sores shall not stand test of time in your life. Bleeds shall end, while wounds are cured.

PRAYER POINTS

1. Full life restoration and healing come into my life in the name of Jesus.
2. Lord Jesus, be at the center of my physical being.

3. Every attack against my brain be nullified, in the name of Jesus.

4. O Lord, heal the wound in my heart, in the name of Jesus.

5. Social disorder affecting my family and others, be healed.

6. Every inner pain inflicted on me in my childhood, be healed in the name of Jesus.

7. In the name of Jesus I am healed

8. Every spiritual maggot in my life die and dry up in the name of Jesus.

9. Balm of Gilead, heal my wound in the name of Jesus.

10. Holy Spirit, heal my infirmity in the name of Jesus.

11. I dismantle altars of sickness and disease raised against my health.

12. Authority of darkness over my life, scatter in the name of Jesus.

13. Every bondage that enslaved me, break in the name of Jesus.

14. O Lord, take away from me all sickness in the name of Jesus.

15. O Lord, forgive me all my iniquities and heal my disease.

16. Lord Jesus, make me whole.

17. Lord Jesus, heal me by your stripes.

18. With God all things are possible, so I am healed.

19. Wicked spirit, loose your hold and set me free in the name of Jesus.

20. I receive divine healing for breakthrough and success in the name of Jesus.

21. I break the law of sickness and death over my life.

22. O Lord, heal the water and blood in my body.

23. My nerves and vain receive healing in the name of Jesus.

24. O Lord, let me experience divine healing from my head to my sole in the name of Jesus.

25. Bruises and sores shall not stand test of time in my life, in the name of Jesus.

26. Today, bleeds shall end, while wounds shall cure in my life, in the name of Jesus.

27. My God shall take away burden, sorrow and mourning in my life, in the name of Jesus.

28. Lord Jesus, heal every disappointment in my life.

29. Lord Jesus, heal my past life and fill every void in my life.

30. Lord Jesus, heal every department of my life.

31. Testimony of Christ, laugh and praises are mine in the name of Jesus.

32. Every crisis in my heart, receive deliverance.

33. O Lord, gladden my heart with good health.

CHAPTER TEN

WHEN OFFICE SEEMS TOUGH AND HOT...CALL PSALM 121

The best therapy is to wait on the Lord in the midst of confusion, not rush at taking decision. Many want to direct God, instead of resigning to faith and be directed by God; to show him way, instead of passively following his leads.

Office that brings goodness is likely to be hot. In such place, gang up, backbiting, fear, calamity, attacks etc. may not be found wanting.

Take the ministry of our Lord Jesus as an example; for forty days and nights, he was kept in the presence of Satan in the wilderness. Under circumstances of special trial, he prevails, giving Satan hard knocks of his life. The three Hebrew children were not left out, they were kept a season amid furnace heated seven times more than it was to be heated. They saw death in the course of spiritual officialdom and conquered it. In the midst of flame they were calm; and composed in the presence of the tyrants last appliances of torture. They never lost hope, rather hardened their hearts against failure and submission to circumstance. They felt the presence of God and won. What about Daniel? All live long might he set among the lions, and when he set among the lions, and when he was taken up out of the then, "no manner of hurt was found upon him, because he believed in his God" They dwelt in the presence of the enemy because they dwelt in the presence of God.

Brethren, never doubt God. Never say was he unsympathetic of your situation. I want you to realize one thing, no situation is permanent; you won't be enslaved by circumstances. The longest day at last rings out the evening song of joy. Weeping may endure for a night; joy comes in the morning; after darkness comes light.

It is time to rely on God even in the midst of problems. The battle to dwell and win in hot environment connotes having table in the midst of enemies, walking in the valley of shadow of death unmolested, a shelter from the storm, a fortress amidst the foe, a life preserved in the face of continual pressure. What you need most is grace of Christ to be sufficient for you, and make you victorious in the hardest places.

We often pray to be delivered from calamities, but don't pray to be made what we should be, in the very presence of the calamities, to live amid them, as long as they lost, to be sheltered by God, and can therefore remain in the midst of them, so long as they continue, without any hurt.

Where do you occupy in office, lower, middle or upper cadre of the ladder? One thing is certain wherever you may occupy; there are rooms for upper springs to flow into your life. There are springs that flow in the low places, in the hard places, in the desert places, in the lone places, in the common places, and no matter what, your spring shall find you out.

Most times, you need unfailing springs that heal the heart for great harvest; you should conquer circumstances for your star to shine. Dedication to work, ability to read signs on the wall, clarity of mind, accountability, good character and ability to pray are platforms to excel in life.

No matter what, it is the seed of greatness in you, your employer needs. Wake the seed of greatness in you. Everything that makes you great is built and planted inside of you. It is left to you, to rise up to situation. You can be great in the face of molestation, or deadly gang up. The uniqueness in you and divine support clears the way. By this, cloud of darkness expires, to a progressive forward match. Do you know, you are too loaded to be a failure? It is time you rule, reign and shine. No matter the challenges, you shall be above not below.

Whatever situation you face study it, don't use human knowledge; rather tell God to lead. He can't lead you into failure. He knows the beginning to the ending. This is why; he is called Alpha and the Omega. He is a Man of Vision; therefore pray for vision that surprise human understanding. Ask God to reveal depth of situation of things, as you may only be seeing the surface. You may think it is hard, yes enduring hardship! Don't shy away from hardship; the Lord is a God of war. The battle may be hard, but here is the exciting part, you will always win if you follow God!

There are strange prayers you can pray when cornered by problems, attacks or calamities. The prayer should Centre on power to live above problems and presence of God at critical times. It is not good enough to pray, that your company should fold up, or staff to die, but to pray and excel in the face of all odds.

In the midst of situations, we need to pray. Our prayers are God's opportunities. Are you in gladness? Prayer can turn your affliction sweet and strengthening. Are you in extreme danger from outward or inward enemies? Prayer can set at your right hand an angel whose touch could shatter a millstone into smaller dust than the flour it grinds. What more? The glance of angels could lay battalion of army low!

God leads his people in war because we must fight what is good and right. Your faith is to work to earn good living. But there you are, enemies stood firm against us, demonstrating and boasting where we will pass? In 1Timothy 6:12, Paul teaches that we are to fight the good fight of faith. You must fight to establish your faith. The fight is not physical but spiritual.

The people who fight against the problems and trials of life are not the ones with weak faith, but one with strong faith. With faith you fight for healing, when healing doesn't seem to be there. It is fighting for promotion, when promotion seems far way. It is fighting unemployment when sack and lay off is rampant in the work place. It is fight for peace when every side is riotous. You are a fighter of good faith, when you say, "I shall not lose my job, if everyone loses his/hers". "I shall not be defeated in the market square of labour market". "I shall fight with everything I have to establish peace and greatness of my lineage" This is faith for you.

Prayer is spiritual fight, and if we don't, we shall never be victorious. If we never have victory, we will never have peace. And if there is no peace, how can we handle office? So we fight until we win, then we enjoy victory, and take peace, and comfort because the battle has been won. Then you get strengthened for the next battle, which is promotion. The fact that the going is difficult does not mean that you are not of the will of God. But then, it is time to perform more, do more, work harder and better.

May God bless you and promote you. Make haste and phone God for a greater height.

PRAYER POINTS

1. O Lord, make me a fighter of good faith in the name of Jesus.
2. O Lord, give me faith to pray and fight until I win every battle around me.
3. O Lord, give me power to pray and excel in face of all odds, in the name of Jesus.

4. Angels of God guide me 24 hours every day against temptations and attack in the name of Jesus.

5. Every charm targeted against me catch fire and roast to ashes.

6. Wicked padlock fashion against my promotion and employment, break and scatter.

7. Every wickedness promoting demotion in my life, die in the name of Jesus.

8. My fears fall upon my enemies and let them surrender in the name of Jesus.

9. My mouth shall reduce my enemy to nothing in the name of Jesus.

10. I shall not be identified with shame in the name of Jesus.

11. Failure shall not be my portion in the name of Jesus.

12. Spirit of demotion assign to pull me down, die in the name of Jesus.

13. Every tormentor assign to deal with me in office, be rendered useless in the name of Jesus.

14. Every gang up targeted against me scatter in the name of Jesus.

15. Every dark altar visited in other to harm me catch fire and roast to ashes in the name of Jesus.

16. Fears of office in my heart expire in the name of Jesus.

17. O God, raise an enemy against my enemies and let them scatter.

18. Every attack against me in office scatter in the name of Jesus.

19. Calamities awaiting me in office scatter in the name of Jesus.

20. O Lord, let my weep end today in the name of Jesus.

21. Goodness of God, locate me on every side, in the name of Jesus.

22. Wasters and emptier of destiny in the corridor of my life, die in the name of Jesus.

23. Every battle against me in office scatter in the name of Jesus.

24. I enter into my season of possession in the name of Jesus.

25. People shall gather at my result and celebrate with me in the name of Jesus.

26. Anything planted in my life to make me useless before my employer, die and rise no more.

27. Breakthrough is my birthright, I will move forward and succeed, in the name of Jesus.

28. Enemy shall not take over the table of my existence, in the name of Jesus.

29. Every darkness hovering over my life expire in the name of Jesus.

30. Even I walk in the shadow of death, I will remain unmolested in the name of Jesus.

31. My foes shall meet double destruction in the name of Jesus.

32. My fasting and prayer shall not be in vain, in the name of Jesus.

33. Songs and praises in my mouth shall not seize, in the name of Jesus.

YOU HAVE BATTLES TO WIN
TRY THESE BOOKS

1. <u>COMMAND THE DAY: DAILY PRAYER BOOK</u>

Each day of the week is loaded with meanings and divine assurance. God did not create each day of the week for the fun of it. Blessings, success, gifts, resources, hopes, portfolios, duties, rights, prophecies, warnings and challenges, are loaded in each day.

Do you know the language, command or decree you can use to claim what belongs to you in each day of the week? Do you know in Christendom, Monday can be equated to one of the days of creation in Genesis chapter one? Do you know creation lasted for six days and God rested on the seventh day? What day of the week can Christian equate as the first day of the week, if we follow Christian calendar? What day can we call day seven?

This book shall give insight to these questions. It shall explain how you can command each day of the week according to creation in the book of Genesis chapter one.

Above all, you shall exercise your right and claim what is hidden in each day of the week.
Check for this in <u>COMMAND THE DAY: DAILY PRAYER BOOK</u>

2. <u>PRAYER TO REMEMBER DREAMS</u>

A lot of people are passing through this spiritual epidemic on a daily basis. Their dream life is epileptic, having no ability to remember all dreams they dream, or sometimes forget everything entirely. This is nothing but spiritual havoc you need to erase from your spiritual record.
The answer to every form of spiritual blackout caused by spiritual erasers is found in, <u>PRAYER TO REMEMBER DREAMS</u>

3. <u>100% CONFESSIONS AND PROPHECIES TO LOCATE HELPERS AND HELPERS TO LOCATE YOU</u>

This is a wonderful book on confessions and prophecies to locate helpers and helpers to locate you. It is a prayer book loaded with over two thousand (2,000) prayer points.

The book unravels how to locate unknown helpers, prayers to arrest mind of helpers and prayers for manifestation after encounter with helpers.

4. ANOINTING FOR ELEVENTH HOUR HELP: HOPE AND HELP FOR YOUR TURBULENT TIMES

This book tells much of what to do at injury hour called eleventh hour. When you read and use this book as prescribed fear shall vanish in your life when pursuing a project, career or contract.

5. PRAYER TO LOCATE HELPERS AND HELPERS TO LOCATE YOU

Our divine helper is God. He created us to be together and be of help to one another. In the midst of no help we lost out, ending our journey in the wilderness.

There are keys assign to open right doors of life. You need right key to locate your helpers. Enough is enough; of suffering in silence.

With this book, you shall locate your helpers while your helpers shall locate you.

6. FIRE FOR FIRE PART ONE: (PRAYER BOOK BOOK 1)

This prayer book is fast at answering spiritual problems. It is a bulldozer prayer book, full of prayers all through. It is highly recommended for night vigil. Testimonies are pouring in daily from users of this book across the world!

7. PRAYER FOR FRUIT OF THE WOMB: EXPECTING MOTHERS

This prayer book is children magnet. By faith and believe in God Almighty, as soon as you use this book open doors to child bearing shall be yours. Amen

8. PRAYER FOR PREGNANT WOMEN: WITH ALL CHRISTIAN NAMES AND MEANINGS

This is a spiritual prayer book loaded with prayers of solution for pregnant women. As soon as you take in, the prayers you shall pray from day one of conception to the day of delivery are written in this book.

9. WARFARE IN THE OFFICE: PRAYER TO SILENCE TOUGH TIMES IN OFFICE

It is high time you pray prayers of power must change hands in office. Use this book and liberate yourself from every form of office yoke.

10. MY MARRIAGE SHALL NOT BREAK: THE SECRET TO LOVE AND MARRIAGE THAT LASTS

Marriage is corner piece of life, happiness and joy. You need to hold it tight and guide it from wicked intruders and destroyer of homes.

11. VICTORY OVER SATANIC HOUSE PART ONE: RIDDING YOUR HOME OF SPIRITUAL DARKNESS

Are you a tenant, Land lord bombarded left and right, front and back by wicked people around you?
With this book you shall be liberated from the hooks of the enemy.

12. DICTIONARY OF DREAMS: THE DREAM INTERPRETATION

DICTIONARY WITH SYMBOLS, SIGNS, AND MEANINGS

This is a must book for every home. It gives accurate details to about **10,000 (Ten thousand) dreams and interpretations,** written in alphabetical order for quick reference and easy digestion. The book portrays spiritual revelations with sound prophetic guidelines. It is loaded with Biblical references and violent prayers.
Ask for yours today.

For Further Enquiries Contact
THE AUTHOR
EVANGELIST TELLA OLAYERI
P.O. Box 1872 Shomolu Lagos.
Tel: +2348023583168

FROM AUTHOR'S DESK

BEFORE YOU GO

Hello,

Thank you for purchasing this book. Would you consider posting a review about this book? In addition to providing feedback and arousing others into Christ's bosom, reviews can help other customers to know about the book.

Please take a minute to leave a review on this book.

I would appreciate that!

Thank you in advance, for your review and your patronage!!

If you would like to leave a review on my other books click the link below.

https://tellaolayeri.com/review.php

NOTE: You can get all my books from my website www.tellaolayeri.com

SHARE YOUR TESTIMONY

We love testimonies. We love to hear what God has done for you, your family, your business etc. as you draw close to Him in prayer. Please share your testimony with us.

https://tellaolayeri.com/testimony.php

NOTE: If you want your picture to be shown with your testimony send it to tellaolayeri@gmail.com

I also invite you to checkout our website at www.tellaolayeri.com and consider joining our newsletter (get free six powerful book) which we send out once in a while with great tips, testimonies and revelations from God's Word for a victorious living.

Feel free to drop us your prayer request. We will join faith with you and God's power will be released in your life and issue in question.

www.tellaolayeri.com/prayerrequest.php

GOOD NEWS!!!

My audiobook is now available, to get one visit **audible**.

If you are reading from my paperback visit **acx.com** and search **"Tella Olayeri."**

Brethren, to be loaded and reloaded visit: *amazon.com/author/tellaolayeri* for a full spiritual sojourn for my books.

Thanks.

DONATE TO THE MINISTRY

Why Give?

We have two major area of focus: The less Privileged and Charity.

Service to people and help to set up outstanding Modern Printing Press to reach thousands for free evangelism pamphlets and books to hinterland and the needy.

To achieve this, financial support is needed and we count you as one to support this ministry. A drop of water makes an ocean.

No donation is small or little. Donate through any of the ways listed below. May God bless your purse and source. Amen.

DONATE IN NAIRA

Bank Name: Guaranty Trust Bank Plc.

Account Name: OLAYERI ADIKU TELLA

Account Number: 0499255414

DONATE IN DOLLARS

Bank Name: Guaranty Trust Bank Plc.

Account Name: OLAYERI ADIKU TELLA

Account Number: 0499255098

Swift code: GTBINGLA

Visit the donation page on my website to donate online:

www.tellaolayeri.com/donate.php

ABOUT THE AUTHOR

Tella Olayeri grew from Spiritual Warrior to Spiritual Warlord in the Vineyard of God. His books have changed lives of millions, with banner of praises and testimonies in their hands!

He is a solution giver to problems and challenges men and women pass through on daily basis. He frowns at satanic oppression and demonic agenda propagated by powers of darkness. He is known for his wonderful deliverance books that address, swallow and bring abrupt end to fierce attacks of the enemy. **"Wonders and miracles"**, connotes his deliverance books.

Tella's books are globally read and accepted, based on operation "do-it-yourself". His books are instant solution to problems laced with fire prayer missiles that give instant deliverance to demonic yoke and oppression, health hazards, witchcraft attacks etc. His books will teach your hands to wage war and your fingers to fight against forces of darkness.

Tella Olayeri is a role model in Christian warfare. He is a Counselor and Preacher of the Word. His writings are wonderful and courageous for Christian soldiers in the battle of life to harvest breakthrough, salvation, spiritual protection, open doors and miracles.

One of his major research book is **DICTIONARY OF DREAMS**, that gives instant relief to millions of how to interpret dreams. The book has about ten thousand (10,000) dreams with accurate interpretations.

Tella Olayeri is happily married to his wife, Sister Ngozi Judith Olayeri. The marriage is blessed with five children, Miss Ibukun, David, Michael, Miss Comfort and Miss Mercy.

Connect with Tella Olayeri at www.tellaolayeri.com to receive powerful daily message.

www.ingramcontent.com/pod-product-compliance
Lightning Source LLC
Chambersburg PA
CBHW051423150726
48000CB00005B/1929